The Golden Goose

In a small village by the forest there lived a man and his wife. They had three sons. The elder sons were hard working while the youngest, though he too worked hard, was called Dummling. He was mocked at by everyone in the village due to his name. One day, the old man called his eldest son and said, 'Son, fetch some hew wood from the forest.' Before he went, his mother gave him a beautiful sweet cake to eat and a bottle of wine to drink.

When the eldest son was walking through the forest, he met a little grey-haired old man. The old man greeted him and said, 'Son, do give me a piece of cake, and let me have a draught of your wine for I am very hungry and thirsty.' 'I cannot do that,' said the eldest son. 'If I do so, I shall have nothing to eat and drink myself. Go away!' The next moment, the eldest son turned on his heel and went on his way.

Soon, while bringing down a hew tree, the eldest son made a false stroke, and the axe cut him in the arm. He had to return home empty-handed. All this was the little grey man's doing.

When his eldest son had returned home hurt, the old man sent his second son to the forest. His mother gave him too, like the eldest, a cake and a bottle of wine. He also met the little grey-haired man in the forest. 'Son, give me some food,' he said. 'I am hungry and thirsty.' He, too, like his elder brother refused him.

His punishment, however, was not delayed. When he had made a few blows at the tree he struck himself in the leg. Later with some help, he reached home limping.

It was then Dummling said, 'Father, let me go to the forest to bring wood.' But his father said, 'Your brothers have hurt themselves. You shall not go. You are not very efficient either.' But Dummling continued to plead to his father. In the end, his father agreed to let him go. But unlike his brothers, he only got a cinder cake and a bottle of sour beer.

When Dummling came to the forest, he too like his elder brothers met the little old grey-haired man. The old man greeted him and said, ‘Give me a piece of your cake and a drink out of your bottle; I am so hungry and thirsty.’

Dummling replied, ‘I have only cinder-cake and sour beer, if that pleases you, we will sit down and eat.’ When Dummling pulled out his cinder-cake, it became a fine sweet cake, and the sour beer turned into good wine.

When the old man and Dummling had eaten and drank, the old man said, 'Since you have a good heart and are willing to share what you have, I will give you good luck. There stands an old tree, cut it down, and you will find something at its roots.' Saying so, the little man took his leave.

Dummling went and cut down the tree just as the old man had told him too. As the tree fell, Dummling saw a goose sitting at the roots of the tree with feathers of pure gold.

Dummling then picked up the goose and thought of spending the night in an inn before starting for his home. Now, the owner of the inn had three daughters, who had seen the goose and were curious to know what such a wonderful bird might be. The three girls also wanted to have one of its golden feathers.
The eldest daughter thought, 'I shall soon find an opportunity to pull out a feather.' So, as soon as Dummling had gone out of his room, she seized the goose by the wing, but her finger and hand remained stuck fast to it.

She didn't know what to do. Minutes later, the second sister came, thinking only of how she might get a feather for herself. But she, too, had hardly touched the goose and she was held fast to it. The youngest sister, too, got stuck to the goose for she did not listen to her sisters' warnings. So, the three sisters spent their night stuck to the goose.

When the Dummling saw the three sisters, he said nothing but fell asleep. Next morning, he took the goose under his arm and set out, without troubling himself about the three girls who were hanging on to the goose. The sisters had no other option but to go with the Dummling and his goose.

While they were crossing the fields, they met a parson. When he saw the procession, he cried, 'Shame on you girls, why are you running along with this young man?'

Saying so, the parson grabbed the arm of the youngest and tried to pull her away. But no sooner had he touched her that he too was stuck and was obliged to run behind them. In no time, a sexton and two labourers too got stuck to the others as they tried to get the sexton and parson free. What a funny sight it was!

CITY

Soon, they all came to a city. Here, the ruling king had a daughter who was so serious that no one could make her laugh. So, he had put forth a decree that whosoever shall make her laugh shall marry her. When Dummling heard this, he went with his goose and his train before the king's daughter. No sooner had she seen them that she burst out laughing.

The decree had been fulfilled. But the king did not like Dummling. To get rid of him, the king said, 'First bring me a man who can drink a cellarful of wine.'

It was then that Dummling thought of the little grey-haired man. At once, he returned to the forest and found the old man sitting under a tree looking sorrowful. Dummling asked him, 'Why are you so sorrowful?' 'I am terribly thirsty,' said the old man. 'I have emptied a barrel of wine but that seems like a drop of wine.'

Hearing this, Dummling said, ‘I can help you. Come with me and you shall be satisfied.’ He then led the grey-haired man to the king’s cellar. By evening, to the king’s great surprise, all the wine barrels in his cellar were empty.

‘I shall now get the princess’ hand in marriage,’ said the Dummling. But the king did not want to marry the princess to him. So, he thought of a new condition.

'Find me a man who can eat a whole mountain of bread,' said the king. Immediately, Dummling went to the old grey-haired man in the forest. The man had tied his body in straps and looked awful. Seeing Dummling, he said, 'I have eaten ovenful of rolls but my hunger is not quenched.'

Dummling gladly said, 'Come with me and you shall have plenty to eat.' The old grey-haired man ate a mountain of bread by evening.

Though Dummling had kept his word, the king said, 'Bring me a ship that can sail on land and on water and you shall marry the princess.'

Yet again, Dummling returned to the old grey-haired man. The old man said, 'Since you have given me to eat and drink, I will give you the ship that could sail on sea and on land.' When the king saw the ship, he could no longer prevent Dummling from marrying his daughter. So, Dummling married the king's daughter and lived a contented life.